C000177232

Every Day Matters

2024 Diary

A Year of Inspiration for the Mind, Body and Spirit

Created by
Jess Sharp
as seen on Instagram
@jessrachelsharp

WATKINS
Sharing Wisdom
Since 1893

Every Day Matters 2024 Diary

First published in UK and USA in 2023 by
Watkins, an imprint of Watkins Media Limited
Unit 11, Shepperton House
89–93 Shepperton Road
London N1 3DF

enquiries@watkinspublishing.com

Designed by Watkins Media Limited

Commissioning Editor: Lucy Carroll
Assistant Editor: Brittany Willis
Illustrator and Author: Jess Sharp
Head of Design: Karen Smith
Designer: Kieryn Tyler

Desk Diary ISBN: 978-178678-755-2
Pocket Diary ISBN: 978-178678-756-9

Printed in China

Signs of the Zodiac:

♒	Aquarius	January 20–February 18
♓	Pisces	February 19–March 19
♈	Aries	March 20–April 19
♉	Taurus	April 20–May 20
♊	Gemini	May 21–June 20
♋	Cancer	June 21–July 21
♌	Leo	July 22–August 22
♍	Virgo	August 23–September 22
♎	Libra	September 23–October 22
♏	Scorpio	October 23–November 21
♐	Sagittarius	November 22–December 20
♑	Capricorn	December 21–January 19

Phases of the Moon:

- ● New moon
- ☽ First quarter
- ○ Full moon
- ☾ Last quarter

Abbreviations:

BCE: Before Common Era (equivalent of BC)
CE: Common Era (equivalent of AD)
UK: United Kingdom
SCO: Scotland
NIR: Northern Ireland
ROI: Republic of Ireland
CAN: Canada
USA: United States of America
NZ: New Zealand
AUS: Australia
ACT: Australian Capital Territory
NSW: New South Wales
NT: Northern Territory
QLD: Queensland
SA: South Australia
TAS: Tasmania
VIC: Victoria
WA: Western Australia

Publisher's Notes:

All dates relating to the zodiac signs and the
phases of the moon are based on Greenwich
Mean Time (GMT).

All North American holiday dates are based
on Eastern Standard Time (EST).

Jewish and Islamic holidays begin at sundown
on the date given. Islamic holidays may vary by
a day or two, as the Islamic calendar is based on
a combination of actual sightings of the moon
and astronomical calculations.

Watkins Media Limited cannot accept
responsibility for any injuries or damage
incurred as a result of following the information,
exercises or therapeutic techniques contained
in this book.

Dates were correct at the time of going to press.

2023

JANUARY
M	TU	W	TH	F	SA	SU
						1
2	3	4	5	6	7	8
9	10	11	12	13	14	15
16	17	18	19	20	21	22
23	24	25	26	27	28	29
30	31					

FEBRUARY
M	TU	W	TH	F	SA	SU
		1	2	3	4	5
6	7	8	9	10	11	12
13	14	15	16	17	18	19
20	21	22	23	24	25	26
27	28					

MARCH
M	TU	W	TH	F	SA	SU
		1	2	3	4	5
6	7	8	9	10	11	12
13	14	15	16	17	18	19
20	21	22	23	24	25	26
27	28	29	30	31		

APRIL
M	TU	W	TH	F	SA	SU
					1	2
3	4	5	6	7	8	9
10	11	12	13	14	15	16
17	18	19	20	21	22	23
24	25	26	27	28	29	30

MAY
M	TU	W	TH	F	SA	SU
1	2	3	4	5	6	7
8	9	10	11	12	13	14
15	16	17	18	19	20	21
22	23	24	25	26	27	28
29	30	31				

JUNE
M	TU	W	TH	F	SA	SU
			1	2	3	4
5	6	7	8	9	10	11
12	13	14	15	16	17	18
19	20	21	22	23	24	25
26	27	28	29	30		

JULY
M	TU	W	TH	F	SA	SU
					1	2
3	4	5	6	7	8	9
10	11	12	13	14	15	16
17	18	19	20	21	22	23
24	25	26	27	28	29	30
31						

AUGUST
M	TU	W	TH	F	SA	SU
	1	2	3	4	5	6
7	8	9	10	11	12	13
14	15	16	17	18	19	20
21	22	23	24	25	26	27
28	29	30	31			

SEPTEMBER
M	TU	W	TH	F	SA	SU
				1	2	3
4	5	6	7	8	9	10
11	12	13	14	15	16	17
18	19	20	21	22	23	24
25	26	27	28	29	30	

OCTOBER
M	TU	W	TH	F	SA	SU
						1
2	3	4	5	6	7	8
9	10	11	12	13	14	15
16	17	18	19	20	21	22
23	24	25	26	27	28	29
30	31					

NOVEMBER
M	TU	W	TH	F	SA	SU
		1	2	3	4	5
6	7	8	9	10	11	12
13	14	15	16	17	18	19
20	21	22	23	24	25	26
27	28	29	30			

DECEMBER
M	TU	W	TH	F	SA	SU
				1	2	3
4	5	6	7	8	9	10
11	12	13	14	15	16	17
18	19	20	21	22	23	24
25	26	27	28	29	30	31

2024

JANUARY
M	TU	W	TH	F	SA	SU
1	2	3	4	5	6	7
8	9	10	11	12	13	14
15	16	17	18	19	20	21
22	23	24	25	26	27	28
29	30	31				

FEBRUARY
M	TU	W	TH	F	SA	SU
			1	2	3	4
5	6	7	8	9	10	11
12	13	14	15	16	17	18
19	20	21	22	23	24	25
26	27	28	29			

MARCH
M	TU	W	TH	F	SA	SU
				1	2	3
4	5	6	7	8	9	10
11	12	13	14	15	16	17
18	19	20	21	22	23	24
25	26	27	28	29	30	31

APRIL
M	TU	W	TH	F	SA	SU
1	2	3	4	5	6	7
8	9	10	11	12	13	14
15	16	17	18	19	20	21
22	23	24	25	26	27	28
29	30					

MAY
M	TU	W	TH	F	SA	SU
		1	2	3	4	5
6	7	8	9	10	11	12
13	14	15	16	17	18	19
20	21	22	23	24	25	26
27	28	29	30	31		

JUNE
M	TU	W	TH	F	SA	SU
					1	2
3	4	5	6	7	8	9
10	11	12	13	14	15	16
17	18	19	20	21	22	23
24	25	26	27	28	29	30

JULY
M	TU	W	TH	F	SA	SU
1	2	3	4	5	6	7
8	9	10	11	12	13	14
15	16	17	18	19	20	21
22	23	24	25	26	27	28
29	30	31				

AUGUST
M	TU	W	TH	F	SA	SU
			1	2	3	4
5	6	7	8	9	10	11
12	13	14	15	16	17	18
19	20	21	22	23	24	25
26	27	28	29	30	31	

SEPTEMBER
M	TU	W	TH	F	SA	SU
						1
2	3	4	5	6	7	8
9	10	11	12	13	14	15
16	17	18	19	20	21	22
23	24	25	26	27	28	29
30						

OCTOBER
M	TU	W	TH	F	SA	SU
	1	2	3	4	5	6
7	8	9	10	11	12	13
14	15	16	17	18	19	20
21	22	23	24	25	26	27
28	29	30	31			

NOVEMBER
M	TU	W	TH	F	SA	SU
				1	2	3
4	5	6	7	8	9	10
11	12	13	14	15	16	17
18	19	20	21	22	23	24
25	26	27	28	29	30	

DECEMBER
M	TU	W	TH	F	SA	SU
						1
2	3	4	5	6	7	8
9	10	11	12	13	14	15
16	17	18	19	20	21	22
23	24	25	26	27	28	29
30	31					

2025

JANUARY
M	TU	W	TH	F	SA	SU
		1	2	3	4	5
6	7	8	9	10	11	12
13	14	15	16	17	18	19
20	21	22	23	24	25	26
27	28	29	30	31		

FEBRUARY
M	TU	W	TH	F	SA	SU
					1	2
3	4	5	6	7	8	9
10	11	12	13	14	15	16
17	18	19	20	21	22	23
24	25	26	27	28		

MARCH
M	TU	W	TH	F	SA	SU
					1	2
3	4	5	6	7	8	9
10	11	12	13	14	15	16
17	18	19	20	21	22	23
24	25	26	27	28	29	30
31						

APRIL
M	TU	W	TH	F	SA	SU
	1	2	3	4	5	6
7	8	9	10	11	12	13
14	15	16	17	18	19	20
21	22	23	24	25	26	27
28	29	30				

MAY
M	TU	W	TH	F	SA	SU
			1	2	3	4
5	6	7	8	9	10	11
12	13	14	15	16	17	18
19	20	21	22	23	24	25
26	27	28	29	30	31	

JUNE
M	TU	W	TH	F	SA	SU
						1
2	3	4	5	6	7	8
9	10	11	12	13	14	15
16	17	18	19	20	21	22
23	24	25	26	27	28	29
30						

JULY
M	TU	W	TH	F	SA	SU
	1	2	3	4	5	6
7	8	9	10	11	12	13
14	15	16	17	18	19	20
21	22	23	24	25	26	27
28	29	30	31			

AUGUST
M	TU	W	TH	F	SA	SU
				1	2	3
4	5	6	7	8	9	10
11	12	13	14	15	16	17
18	19	20	21	22	23	24
25	26	27	28	29	30	31

SEPTEMBER
M	TU	W	TH	F	SA	SU
1	2	3	4	5	6	7
8	9	10	11	12	13	14
15	16	17	18	19	20	21
22	23	24	25	26	27	28
29	30					

OCTOBER
M	TU	W	TH	F	SA	SU
		1	2	3	4	5
6	7	8	9	10	11	12
13	14	15	16	17	18	19
20	21	22	23	24	25	26
27	28	29	30	31		

NOVEMBER
M	TU	W	TH	F	SA	SU
					1	2
3	4	5	6	7	8	9
10	11	12	13	14	15	16
17	18	19	20	21	22	23
24	25	26	27	28	29	30

DECEMBER
M	TU	W	TH	F	SA	SU
1	2	3	4	5	6	7
8	9	10	11	12	13	14
15	16	17	18	19	20	21
22	23	24	25	26	27	28
29	30	31				

2024 International Public Holidays

Argentina	Jan 1, Feb 12–13, Mar 24, Mar 29, Apr 2, May 1, May 25, Jun 17, Jun 20, Jul 9, Aug 19, Oct 14, Nov 18, Dec 8, Dec 25
Australia	Jan 1, Jan 26, Mar 4 (WA), Mar 11 (TAS, VIC, ACT, SA), Mar 29, Mar 30 (exc TAS, NT), Mar 31 (QLD, WA, VIC), Apr 1, Apr 2, Apr 25, May 6 (NT, QLD), Jun 3 (WA), Aug 5 (NT), Oct 7 (ACT, NSW, QLD, SA), Dec 24–25, Dec 26 (exc SA), Dec 31 (NT, SA)
Austria	Jan 1, Jan 6, Apr 1, May 1, May 9, May 20, May 30, Aug 15, Oct 26, Nov 1, Dec 8, Dec 25–26
Belgium	Jan 1, Apr 1, May 1, May 9, May 20, Jul 21, Aug 15, Nov 1, Nov 11, Dec 25
Brazil	Jan 1, Mar 29, Apr 21, May 1, Sep 7, Oct 12, Nov 2, Nov 15, Dec 25
Canada	Jan 1, Mar 29, Apr 1, May 20, Jul 1, Aug 5, Sep 2, Sep 30, Oct 14, Nov 11, Dec 25–26
China	Jan 1, Feb 9–15, Apr 4–5, Apr 29–May 1, Jun 10, Sep 17–18, Oct 1–7
Denmark	Jan 1, Mar 28–Apr 1, Apr 26, May 9, May 19–20, Dec 25–26
Finland	Jan 1, Jan 6, Mar 29–Apr 1, May 1, May 9, May 19, Jun 21–22, Nov 2, Dec 6, Dec 24–26
France	Jan 1, Mar 29, Apr 1, May 1, May 8, May 9, May 19–20, Jul 14, Aug 15, Nov 1, Nov 11, Dec 25
Germany	Jan 1, Mar 29, Apr 1, May 1, May 9, May 20, May 30, Oct 3, Dec 25–26
Greece	Jan 1, Jan 6, Mar 18, Mar 25, May 1, May 3–6, Jun 23–24, Aug 15, Oct 28, Dec 25–26
India	Jan 1, Jan 26, Mar 8, Mar 25, Mar 29, Apr 10, Apr 14, Apr 17, Jun 17, Jul 17, Aug 15, Aug 26, Sep 16, Oct 2, Oct 13, Nov 1, Nov 15, Dec 25
Indonesia	Jan 1, Feb 8, Feb 10, Mar 11, Mar 29, Apr 10, Apr 11, May 1, May 9, May 23, Jun 1, Jun 17, Jul 7, Aug 17, Sep 15, Dec 25
Israel	Apr 23, Apr 29, May 14, Jun 12, Oct 3–4, Oct 12, Oct 17, Oct 24
Italy	Jan 1, Jan 6, Mar 31–Apr 1, Apr 25, May 1, Jun 2, Aug 15, Nov 1, Dec 8, Dec 25–26
Japan	Jan 1, Jan 8, Feb 11–12, Feb 23, Mar 20, Apr 29, May 3–5, Jul 15, Aug 11–12, Sep 16, Sept 22–23, Oct 14, Nov 3–4, Nov 23

Luxembourg	Jan 1, Apr 1, May 1, May 9, May 20, Jun 23, Aug 15, Nov 1, Dec 25–26
Mexico	Jan 1, Feb 5, Mar 18, May 1, Sep 16, Nov 18, Dec 25
Netherlands	Jan 1, Mar 29, Mar 31–Apr 1, Apr 27, May 5, May 9, May 19–20, Dec 25–26
New Zealand	Jan 1–2, Jan 22, Jan 29, Feb 6, Mar 11, Mar 25, Mar 29, Apr 1, Apr 2, Apr 25, Jun 3, Jun 28, Sep 23, Oct 25, Oct 28, Nov 4, Nov 15, Dec 2, Dec 25–26
Nigeria	Jan 1, Mar 29, Apr 1, Apr 10–11, May 1, Jun 12, Jun 16–17, Sep 15, Oct 1, Dec 25–26
Pakistan	Feb 5, Mar 23, Apr 10–12, May 1, Jun 17–18, Jul 16–17, Aug 14, Sep 16, Dec 25
Poland	Jan 1, Jan 6, Mar 31–Apr 1, May 1, May 3, May 19, May 30, Aug 15, Nov 1, Nov 11, Dec 25–26
Portugal	Jan 1, Mar 29, Mar 31, Apr 25, May 1, May 30, Jun 10, Aug 15, Oct 5, Nov 1, Dec 1, Dec 8, Dec 25
Republic of Ireland	Jan 1, Feb 5, Mar 17, Apr 1, May 6, Jun 3, Aug 5, Oct 28, Dec 25–26
Russia	Jan 1–5, Jan 7–8, Feb 23, Mar 8, May 1, May 9, Jun 12, Nov 4
South Africa	Jan 1, Mar 21, Mar 29, Apr 1, Apr 27, May 1, Jun 16–17, Aug 9, Sep 24, Dec 16, Dec 25–26
Spain	Jan 1, Jan 6, Mar 28–29, May 1, Aug 15, Oct 12, Nov 1, Dec 6, Dec 8, Dec 25
Sweden	Jan 1, Jan 6, Mar 29, Mar 31–Apr 1, May 1, May 9, May 19, Jun 6, Jun 22, Nov 2, Dec 25–26
Turkey	Jan 1, Apr 10–12, Apr 23, May 1, May 19, Jun 16–19, Jul 15, Aug 30, Oct 29
United Kingdom	Jan 1, Jan 2 (SCO) , Mar 17–18 (NI), Mar 29, Apr 1, May 6, May 27, Jul 12 (NI), Aug 5 (SCO), Aug 26 (exc SCO), Nov 30 (SCO), Dec 2 (SCO), Dec 25–26
United States	Jan 1, Jan 15, Feb 19, May 27, Jun 19, Jul 4, Sep 2, Oct 14, Nov 11, Nov 28, Dec 25

WELCOME TO 2024!

Hello! How has the past year felt for you?

I hope that, whatever it threw at you, you gave yourself permission to go through it gently. And that you can bring this gentleness with you into the new year that now lies ahead.

As well as giving you plenty of space to organize your daily life in the year to come, this diary offers a positive theme for you to focus on each month. This year's themes are Calm, Hope, Peace, Adventure, Acceptance, Change, Creativity, Love, Courage, Nurturing, Learning and Self-reflection.

Within each of these, you will find a range of thought-provoking weekly quotes and prompts, as well as monthly review questions, all of which aim to help you get the most from the year – whether by reflecting on what has passed, leaning into your hopes and dreams for the future or mindfully savouring what is happening in the present.

My hope is that the pages that follow will help you to connect with yourself on a deeper level. So, here's to 2024 – a year overflowing with potential for exciting new adventures and making more glorious memories!

JANUARY

CALM

In our busy day-to-day lives – in which we often have to rush from one thing to the next – a sense of calm can sometimes feel out of reach.

The din of the external world can leave us feeling drained and longing for respite. So, this month, let's think about how we can create as much calmness in our daily surroundings as possible – so that it can help us feel calmer on the inside, too.

By focusing each week on a different way to make your environment, or everyday routine, feel simpler, calmer, less distracting, less "noisy" and more mindful, you have the power to significantly lessen your stress levels – and therefore boost your overall sense of wellbeing.

Whatever calm looks like for you, I hope you can make some time for it this month and really soak up the goodness it brings. After all, who among us wouldn't benefit from a greater sense of tranquillity in our lives?

AFFIRMATION OF THE MONTH

I am worthy of enjoying
a sense of calm in
my surroundings

JAN 1 – JAN 7
CALM

1 / MONDAY
New Year's Day
Kwanzaa ends

2 / TUESDAY
Public holiday (SCO, NZ)

3 / WEDNESDAY

NOTES

> ## "Life is really simple, but we insist on making it complicated."
>
> CONFUCIUS (c. 551–479 BCE), CHINESE PHILOSOPHER

4 / THURSDAY ☾

5 / FRIDAY
Twelfth Night

6 / SATURDAY
Epiphany

7 / SUNDAY
Christmas Day (Orthodox)

GO TECH-FREE

In an increasingly tech-obsessed world, it's easy to feel like you can never switch off. We have emails, messages and notifications at all hours. This week, create some time without these distractions. Turn off your phone or leave it at home when you go out. Immerse yourself in the tranquillity of just existing for a bit.

JAN 8 – JAN 14
CALM

8 / MONDAY	9 / TUESDAY	10 / WEDNESDAY

NOTES

> ## "Reduce the complexity of life by eliminating the needless wants of life."
>
> EDWIN WAY TEALE (1899–1980), AMERICAN NATURALIST

11 / THURSDAY ●   12 / FRIDAY   13 / SATURDAY

14/ SUNDAY
New Year's Day (Orthodox)

IT'S OKAY TO SAY NO

Saying no can feel tough at times. But if
we're constantly saying yes to everyone and
everything, it means that we are saying no to
any sense of down time and calm in our lives.
This week, say no to something that you don't
particularly want to do or don't have time to
do, and use the time gained for yourself.

JAN 15 – JAN 21
CALM

15 / MONDAY
Martin Luther King Jr. Day

16 / TUESDAY

17 / WEDNESDAY

NOTES

> "I firmly believe that nature brings solace in all troubles."

ANNE FRANK (1929–1945), JEWISH DIARIST

18 / THURSDAY ☽

19 / FRIDAY

20 / SATURDAY ≈

_____
_____
_____
_____
_____
_____

_____
_____
_____
_____

21 / SUNDAY

_____
_____
_____
_____
_____
_____

IMMERSE YOURSELF IN NATURE

Nature is known to nurture us, helping to bring balance and calm to our lives. This week, think of a way you can bring more nature into your life. Whether it's by going for walks in the woods, spending more time in your garden or buying yourself flowers, you can use nature to reconnect with your inner joy and calm.

JAN 22 – JAN 28
CALM

22 / MONDAY

23 / TUESDAY

24 / WEDNESDAY

NOTES

> "Music is the language of the spirit. It opens the secret of life bringing peace, abolishing strife."

KAHLIL GIBRAN (1883–1931), LEBANESE ARTIST AND WRITER

25 / THURSDAY ○
Burns Night (SCO)

26 / FRIDAY
Australia Day

27 / SATURDAY
International Holocaust Remembrance Day

28 / SUNDAY

CREATE A CALMING PLAYLIST

Creating a calm environment doesn't always mean sitting in quietude. It can involve anything that helps you to feel more tranquil. This week, create a playlist of your favourite calming songs. Then, anytime you need a little peaceful grounding, put on your headphones and soak up the relaxing vibes.

JANUARY OVERVIEW

M	TU	W	TH	F	SA	SU
1	2	3	4	5	6	7
8	9	10	11	12	13	14
15	16	17	18	19	20	21
22	23	24	25	26	27	28
29	30	31	1	2	3	4

This month I am grateful for . . .

_____

_____

_____

_____

_____

_____

REFLECTIONS ON CALM

How have you created a more calming environment in your life this month?

How has purposefully curating more of a sense of calm for yourself felt?

What can you do (or stop doing) to bring even more calm into your life in the year to come?

FEBRUARY

HOPE

Life is full of ups and downs that can leave us feeling a little lost in the darkness at times. Hope is a light in that darkness – a gentle hand that can guide us through. It gives us the chance to believe in something bigger than ourselves, to believe in something more. And it reminds us of the possibility of better things to come.

Hope looks different to each person, but it can be found in even the smallest of things if you're willing to look for it, and it can bring the deepest, warmest relief.

It can show up in so many ways: a meal made by a friend when it feels too much to cook for yourself, seeing a rainbow after a storm, noticing the favourite flower of a loved one who's no longer with you or anything else that brings a sense of comfort and reassurance.

Use this month's weekly prompts to help you become more aware of what hope looks like for you and to embrace it in your daily life.

AFFIRMATION OF THE MONTH

I gain strength from hope even in the hardest of times

JAN 29 – FEB 4
HOPE

29 / MONDAY

30 / TUESDAY

31 / WEDNESDAY

NOTES

> "Appreciation can make a day, even change a life. Your willingness to put it into words is all that is necessary."

MARGARET COUSINS (1878–1954), IRISH-INDIAN SUFFRAGIST

1 / THURSDAY

St Brigid's Day (Imbolc)
Black History Month begins
(CAN, USA)

2 / FRIDAY ☾

Candlemas
Groundhog Day

3 / SATURDAY

_____

_____

_____

_____

4 / SUNDAY

_____

_____

_____

_____

_____

_____

EXPRESS YOUR GRATITUDE

Regularly recognizing what we're grateful for
in life can help us to find and hold onto hope.
This week, turn to the Inspired Journalling
section at the back of the diary and make a list
of all the things in life that you feel grateful
for. They don't have to be big things – anything
you are thankful for and that gives you hope.

FEB 5 – FEB 11
HOPE

5 / MONDAY	6 / TUESDAY	7 / WEDNESDAY
	Waitangi Day	

NOTES

> "You cannot have a positive life and a negative mind."

JOYCE MEYER (1943–PRESENT), AMERICAN AUTHOR

8 / THURSDAY

----

9 / FRIDAY ●

----

10 / SATURDAY

Chinese New Year (Year
of the Dragon)
Losar (Tibetan New Year)

----

11 / SUNDAY

LIMIT BAD NEWS INTAKE

Sometimes, if we read or watch a lot of
mainstream news coverage, it can feel like
the world is full of negativity. Remember that
there is also a lot of good out there. This week,
experiment with limiting the amount of "bad"
news that you expose yourself to and seek out
more positive, hopeful news sources instead.

FEB 12 – FEB 18
HOPE

12 / MONDAY
Abraham Lincoln's birthday

13 / TUESDAY

14 / WEDNESDAY
St Valentine's Day
Ash Wednesday

NOTES

> ## "Hope is being able to see that there is light despite all of the darkness."
>
> DESMOND TUTU (1931–2021), SOUTH AFRICAN HUMAN RIGHTS ACTIVIST

15 / THURSDAY
Nirvana Day

16 / FRIDAY ☽

17 / SATURDAY

18 / SUNDAY

LOOK FOR HOPEFUL MOMENTS

Hope can be found in small things all around. This week, keep an eye out for kind acts that restore a sense of hope, and write at least one of them down every night. Doing this will not only help you feel more hopeful, but also allow you to notice good things that come your way in the future.

FEB 19 – FEB 25
HOPE

19 / MONDAY ♓
Presidents' Day

20 / TUESDAY

21 / WEDNESDAY

NOTES

> "At times our own light goes out and is rekindled by a spark from another person."

ALBERT SCHWEITZER (1875–1965), FRENCH-GERMAN PHILOSOPHER

22 / THURSDAY   23 / FRIDAY   24 / SATURDAY ○

25 / SUNDAY

BE SOMEONE'S LIGHT

Hope can often seem like a welcome light in the darkness. This week, think about how you can be that light for someone else. For example, let someone who is going through a tough time know that they are in your thoughts. A simple message saying "I'm here if you need me" can bring a much-needed sense of hope.

FEBRUARY OVERVIEW

M	TU	W	TH	F	SA	SU
29	30	31	1	2	3	4
5	6	7	8	9	10	11
12	13	14	15	16	17	18
19	20	21	22	23	24	25
26	27	28	29	1	2	3

This month I am grateful for . . .

_____

_____

_____

_____

_____

_____

_____

REFLECTIONS ON HOPE

How did you find focusing on the theme of hope this month? And what did you find your greatest sources of hope to be?

In what areas of your life do you feel you need to cultivate more hope at the moment?

How do you think you can help others to find and hold on to more hope?

MARCH

PEACE

We all need comfort in our lives, especially during stressful or difficult times. Comfort is a hug for the soul and a calm, safe harbour from any storms going on around us.

But comfort can mean many different things to different people, depending on our personal likes and needs. As such, we all tend to have our own little ways of self-soothing that we can turn to in times of need. This might be changing into your comfiest clothes after a long day at work; the hug of a loved one or the sound of their voice; listening to your favourite song; watching your favourite film; or the familiar smell of your morning coffee that brings with it a wave of ease. All very different, but all equally important.

Getting to know and being able to tap into your own sources of true comfort in the pages ahead can be a real lifeline, helping you through tough days, as well as boosting your overall happiness and wellbeing.

AFFIRMATION OF THE MONTH

I am worthy of comfort, love and support

FEB 26 – MAR 3
PEACE

26 / MONDAY   27 / TUESDAY   28 / WEDNESDAY

NOTES

> "When the breath wanders the mind is unsteady, but when the breath is calmed, the mind too will be still."

SVĀTMĀRĀMA, 15TH-CENTURY INDIAN YOGI

29 / THURSDAY

1/ FRIDAY
St David's Day

2 / SATURDAY

3 / SUNDAY ☾

BREATHE

Finding peace of mind can be hard when our body isn't feeling at peace. Take a few moments to breathe in deeply through your nose, and as you breathe out through your mouth, give a big sigh – letting anything that's disturbing your peace drift away. Do this as many times as you need to feel more peaceful in both body and mind.

MAR 4 – MAR 10
PEACE

4 / MONDAY
Labour Day (WA)

5 / TUESDAY

6 / WEDNESDAY

NOTES

> "There can be no peace without
> but through peace within."

WILLIAM E. CHANNING (1780–1842), AMERICAN THEOLOGIAN

7 / THURSDAY
World Book Day

8 / FRIDAY
International Women's Day

9 / SATURDAY

---

10 / SUNDAY ●
Mother's Day (UK)
Daylight Saving Time starts
(CAN, USA)
Ramadan begins at sundown

TAKE A MINDFUL SHOWER

Focusing on our senses is a wonderful way to
help us feel more at peace. This week, when you
shower, rather than letting your mind run away,
focus on the feeling of water on your skin, the
sound of the water, the scent of your shower
gel and so on. Savour each feeling, gently
refocusing your mind if and when it wanders.

MAR 11 – MAR 17
PEACE

11 / MONDAY

Commonwealth Day
Public Holiday (ACT, SA,
TAS, VIC)

12 / TUESDAY

13 / WEDNESDAY

NOTES

> ## "There is no new wave, only the sea."
> CLAUDE CHABROL (1930–2010), FRENCH NEW WAVE FILM DIRECTOR

14 / THURSDAY

_____
_____
_____
_____
_____
_____
_____
_____
_____
_____

15 / FRIDAY

_____
_____
_____
_____
_____
_____
_____
_____
_____
_____

16 / SATURDAY

_____
_____
_____
_____

17 / SUNDAY ☽
St Patrick's Day

_____
_____
_____
_____
_____

OBSERVE YOUR THOUGHTS

If you're an overthinker, it can be hard to find
internal peace. This week, imagine your thoughts
are waves on an ocean. You can either swim in
the wave, trying to control them, or you can
watch the sea from the shore, allowing each wave
to rise and fall –recognizing that this is a natural
part of life.

MAR 18 – MAR 24
PEACE

18 / MONDAY
St Patrick's Day observed
(NIR)

19 / TUESDAY

20 / WEDNESDAY ♈
Spring Equinox (UK, ROI,
CAN, USA)
Autumn Equinox (AUS, NZ)

NOTES

> "Peace is not merely a distant goal that we seek, but a means by which we arrive at that goal."

MARTIN LUTHER KING JR. (1929–1968), AMERICAN ACTIVIST

21 / THURSDAY

22 / FRIDAY

23 / SATURDAY
Purim begins at sundown

24 / SUNDAY
Palm Sunday

REMEMBER TO INVEST IN YOURSELF

When things get busy, we can easily forget to invest time in finding peaceful moments. Turn to the Inspired Journalling section at the back of the diary and list the things that help you to feel peaceful. Think about how you could incorporate these into your life more. Try to implement one of these things before the week is over.

MAR 25 – MAR 31
PEACE

25 / MONDAY ○
Holi (Festival of Colours)

26 / TUESDAY

27 / WEDNESDAY

NOTES

> "It's one of the greatest gifts you
> can give yourself, to forgive."

MAYA ANGELOU (1928–2014), AMERICAN POET

28 / THURSDAY
Maundy Thursday

29 / FRIDAY
Good Friday

30 / SATURDAY
Easter Saturday

31 / SUNDAY
Easter Sunday
British Summer Time begins

PEACEFUL SELF-FORGIVENESS

Focusing on things that we feel we should, or
shouldn't, have done can result in never feeling
at peace. This week, identify something that
you're struggling to let go. Gently repeat to
yourself "I forgive myself for ...". The more you
say it, the more you'll believe it, resulting in a
deeper sense of inner peace.

MARCH OVERVIEW

M	TU	W	TH	F	SA	SU
26	27	28	29	1	2	3
4	5	6	7	8	9	10
11	12	13	14	15	16	17
18	19	20	21	22	23	24
25	26	27	28	29	30	31

this month I am grateful for . . .

_____

_____

_____

_____

_____

_____

_____

REFLECTIONS ON PEACE

How has it felt to focus on the theme of inner peace this month?

_____

_____

_____

_____

_____

_____

What activities have helped you to feel more at peace with yourself? And when did you struggle most to feel at peace?

_____

_____

_____

_____

_____

What can you do to create more feelings of peace for yourself in the year to come?

_____

_____

_____

_____

_____

_____

APRIL

ADVENTURE

When did you last feel a sense of adventure in your life? We tend to seek out adventures in abundance when young – climbing trees, going on bike rides and playfully exploring new things. But now that we are adults, our daily routines don't leave much time for mixing things up, which can make us feel a bit stuck, and cause life to feel a bit repetitive.

Reinjecting adventure into our lives can therefore be a wonderful way to break up the monotony of our day-to-day tasks, create some fun, relight a fire within us and make us feel more vibrant and alive again.

Adventure doesn't have to be big or bold; it can be as simple as changing a particular habit, like eating somewhere different to normal or gently pushing yourself to get out of the house and explore somewhere new.

Use the weekly prompts in the pages that follow to help you rediscover your sense of curious exploration – so that every day feels like more of an adventure!

AFFIRMATION OF THE MONTH

Every day I open my
heart to the potential
of new adventures

APR 1 – APR 7
ADVENTURE

1 / MONDAY
Easter Monday
April Fools' Day

2 / TUESDAY ☾

3 / WEDNESDAY

NOTES

> "The purpose of life is to live it ... to reach out eagerly and without fear for newer and richer experience."

ELEANOR ROOSEVELT (1884–1962), AMERICAN POLITICIAN

4 / THURSDAY

5 / FRIDAY

6/ SATURDAY
Laylatul Qadr

_____

7 / SUNDAY

EXPLORE NEW TERRITORY

Injecting a few new things into your life can reignite a sense of adventure. This week, turn to the Inspired Journalling section at the back of the diary and make a list of places that you'd like to visit – new restaurants, art exhibitions, new cities. Start visiting these places and see how it feels to explore new things with an open mind.

APR 8 – APR 14
ADVENTURE

8 / MONDAY ●

9 / TUESDAY
Eid al-Fitr
Ramadan ends at sundown

10 / WEDNESDAY

NOTES

> "Man cannot discover new oceans unless he
> has the courage to lose sight of the shore."

ANDRÉ GIDE (1869–1951), FRENCH AUTHOR

11 / THURSDAY

12 / FRIDAY

13 / SATURDAY

14 / SUNDAY

EMBRACE YOUR FEARS

Sometimes fear – about what could happen or
things that have happened – can stop us being
adventurous. This week, think about what might be
holding you back from enjoying new adventures.
Why do you think these fears are so prominent?
Could you gently face them and allow yourself the
potential to explore new things?

APR 15 – APR 21
ADVENTURE

15 / MONDAY ☽

16 / TUESDAY
Easter (Orthodox)

17 / WEDNESDAY

NOTES

> "Every day is a journey, and the journey itself is home."

MATSUO BASHO (1644–1694), JAPANESE POET

18 / THURSDAY

19 / FRIDAY

20 / SATURDAY ☿

21 / SUNDAY

FIND ADVENTURE IN THE EVERYDAY

Sometimes heading out on an adventure is impractical due to life's responsibilities. This week, have a think about how you can bring more adventure into your life from the comfort of your own home – try a new recipe or a new hobby. Anything goes! If it pushes you out of your comfort zone, then it's an adventure!

APR 22 – APR 28
ADVENTURE

22 / MONDAY
Passover begins at sundown
Earth Day

23 / TUESDAY
St George's Day

24 / WEDNESDAY ○

NOTES

> "The real voyage of discovery consists not in seeking new landscapes but in having new eyes."

MARCEL PROUST (1871–1922), FRENCH AUTHOR

25 / THURSDAY
Anzac Day

26 / FRIDAY

27 / SATURDAY

28 / SUNDAY

ENJOYING THE JOURNEY

Adventures are often as much about the journey as the chosen destination. Have a think about an adventure you recently had – whether a physical trip or an emotional journey. What did you learn about yourself (and your relationship with adventure)? What would you do differently next time?

APRIL OVERVIEW

M	TU	W	TH	F	SA	SU
1	2	3	4	5	6	7
8	9	10	11	12	13	14
15	16	17	18	19	20	21
22	23	24	25	26	27	28
29	30	1	2	3	4	5

This month I am grateful for . . .

_____
_____
_____
_____
_____
_____
_____

REFLECTIONS ON ADVENTURE

What did you do this month to add more adventure to your life?

_____

_____

_____

_____

_____

_____

How did it feel to spend time getting to know your inner adventurer?
Has this shown you a new side to yourself, or have you always been
an adventurous soul?

_____

_____

_____

_____

What will you do to encourage yourself to be more adventurous in the future?

_____

_____

_____

_____

_____

_____

MAY

ACCEPTANCE

How many times have you wished things were different? We often beat ourselves up for things we did, or didn't do, or we fight what we're feeling because we believe we shouldn't be feeling that way.

Learning to accept things as they are, without trying to change them, fight them or wish them away, can be immensely freeing. It allows us to reclaim valuable time and energy that would have otherwise been wasted on worry, doubt and negativity.

Acceptance isn't about forcing yourself to move forward; it's about embracing whatever you are experiencing in the moment and allowing yourself to feel it for as long as you need to. So, if you're feeling sad, feel sad. Accept it, while also trusting that it will pass.

It's not always easy to accept things that come our way, but my hope is that the weekly prompts in the pages that follow will help you with this – and start to allow you to live more authentically and freely.

AFFIRMATION OF THE MONTH

I accept all aspects of my life with grace and compassion

APR 29 – MAY 5
ACCEPTANCE

29 / MONDAY	30 / TUESDAY	1 / WEDNESDAY ☾
		Beltane

NOTES

> "Imperfections are not inadequacies; they are reminders that we're all in this together."

BRENÉ BROWN (1965–PRESENT), AMERICAN PROFESSOR AND AUTHOR

2 / THURSDAY

_____

_____

_____

_____

_____

_____

_____

_____

_____

_____

3 / FRIDAY
Good Friday (Orthodox)

_____

_____

_____

_____

_____

_____

_____

_____

_____

_____

4 / SATURDAY
Easter Saturday (Orthodox)

_____

_____

_____

5 / SUNDAY
Cinco de Mayo
Easter Sunday (Orthodox)

_____

_____

_____

_____

_____

EMBRACE YOUR WHOLE SELF

Few of us like to admit our weaknesses, especially if they're things that other people seem to do effortlessly. This week, write down things you find tough, and then write beside each one: "It's okay to find this hard." Accept that struggles are what make you human and remind yourself that we all have weaknesses.

MAY 6 – MAY 12
ACCEPTANCE

6 / MONDAY
Early May Bank Holiday
(UK, ROI)
Easter Monday (Orthodox)
May Day

7 / TUESDAY

8 / WEDNESDAY ●

NOTES

> ## "Feelings are just visitors.
> ## Let them come and go."

MOOJI (1954–PRESENT), JAMAICAN SPIRITUAL TEACHER

9 / THURSDAY
Ascension Day

10 / FRIDAY

11 / SATURDAY

12 / SUNDAY
Mother's Day (CAN, USA, AUS, NZ)

LET YOUR FEELINGS COME AND GO

How often do you beat yourself up for feeling a certain way? It's only natural to avoid negative emotions at times, but feelings need to be felt in order to be processed. So next time you're trying to resist feeling a certain way, gently remind yourself that this emotion is okay and it's healthy to let your feelings come and go.

MAY 13 – MAY 19
ACCEPTANCE

13 / MONDAY	14 / TUESDAY	15 / WEDNESDAY ☽

NOTES

> "You have power over your mind – not outside
> events. Realize this and you will find strength."

MARCUS AURELIUS (121–180 CE), ROMAN EMPEROR AND PHILOSOPHER

16 / THURSDAY	17 / FRIDAY	18 / SATURDAY

19 / SUNDAY
Pentecost (Whit Sunday)

ACCEPT THE UNCONTROLLABLE

Many things in life are out of our control, and
accepting this can be hard. This week, think
about something that is making you anxious.
Visualize it and kindly say to yourself, "I cannot
control this. All I can control is how I choose to
react to it. So, I choose to accept it with grace
and self-compassion."

MAY 20 – MAY 26
ACCEPTANCE

20/ MONDAY
Whit Monday
Victoria Day (CAN, except
NS, NU, QC)

21 / TUESDAY ♊

22 / WEDNESDAY

NOTES

> "Surrender is the inner transition from resistance to acceptance, from no to yes."

ECKHART TOLLE (1948–PRESENT), GERMAN SPIRITUAL TEACHER

23 / THURSDAY ○
Vesak Day (Buddha Day)

24 / FRIDAY

25 / SATURDAY

26 / SUNDAY
Trinity Sunday

TALK ABOUT IT

Sometimes it's easier to accept things once they are off our chest – a problem shared is a problem halved. This week, try telling someone you trust about something that is bothering you, and see if getting it out in the open aids your acceptance of the issue and lightens the load you are carrying. Talking can be very cathartic.

MAY OVERVIEW

M	TU	W	TH	F	SA	SU
29	30	1	2	3	4	5
6	7	8	9	10	11	12
13	14	15	16	17	18	19
20	21	22	23	24	25	26
27	28	29	30	31	1	2

This month I am grateful for . . .

....
....
....
....
....
....
....

REFLECTIONS ON ACCEPTANCE

How did it feel to focus on the theme of acceptance this month?

_____

_____

_____

_____

_____

_____

What areas of your life have you found yourself practising more acceptance in?

_____

_____

_____

_____

_____

Has focusing on the notion of increased acceptance led you to feel differently about anything or anyone important in your life?

_____

_____

_____

_____

_____

JUNE

CHANGE

How do you approach change? Do you embrace it with arms open, looking forward to a new adventure, or do you find the adjustment hard?

Change often comes with mixed emotions. We can look forward to a change, believe it is the best thing for us, and still find it difficult to navigate. Other times it can happen not through choice but via circumstance and is something we have to work through gently and carefully. Then there are the times we run head first into it and immerse ourselves fully in the joy and freedom it brings.

Change is a tricky thing to navigate, but without it we would never have the opportunity to grow or try new things. It allows us the opportunity to reflect on what has been and use that to form a better future. As long as we honour our feelings and listen to ourselves, change can be a positive step toward a brighter future.

AFFIRMATION OF THE MONTH

It's okay to find change hard, but I know I have got through many changes before and I can do so again

MAY 27 – JUN 2
change

27 / MONDAY
Spring Bank Holiday (UK)
Memorial Day (USA)

28 / TUESDAY

29 / WEDNESDAY

NOTES

> "You can't really change anybody else;
> the only person you can change is you."

KODO NISHIMURA (1989–PRESENT), BUDDHIST MONK AND LGBTQ+ ACTIVIST

30 / THURSDAY ☾
Corpus Christi

31 / FRIDAY

1 / SATURDAY

2 / SUNDAY

HOW DO YOU FIND CHANGE?

How we deal with change differs from person
to person. Some people can embrace it swiftly,
while others find it takes longer to adjust. Think
about your relationship with change. Do you
find it tough? If so, why might this be? Write
down some things you could do to make your
reaction to change more positive and joyful.

JUN 3 – JUN 9
change

3 / MONDAY
Western Australia Day (WA)

4 / TUESDAY

5 / WEDNESDAY

NOTES

> "Focus on your strengths, not your weaknesses."
>
> ROY T. BENNETT (1957–2018), ZIMBABWEAN POLITICIAN

6 / THURSDAY ●

_____
_____
_____
_____
_____

7 / FRIDAY

_____
_____
_____
_____
_____

8 / SATURDAY

_____
_____
_____
_____

9 / SUNDAY

_____
_____
_____
_____
_____

RECOGNIZE YOUR STRENGTHS

Often, when navigating change, we are so busy
feeling anxious that we forget to think about the
strengths we have to help us through. This week,
think about your strengths, whether they be
resilience, humour or organizational skills. Write
down five things you can refer back to as a source
of strength during times of change in the future.

JUN 10 – JUN 16
change

10 / MONDAY	11 / TUESDAY	12 / WEDNESDAY

NOTES

> "The secret of change is to focus all of your energy not on fighting the old, but on building the new."

SOCRATES (c. 470–399 BCE), GREEK PHILOSOPHER

13 / THURSDAY

14 / FRIDAY ☽

15 / SATURDAY

16 / SUNDAY
Father's Day (UK, ROI, CAN, USA)
Eid al-Adha (Feast of the Sacrifice) begins at sundown

TAKE STEPS TOWARD CHANGE

Sometimes we can long for certain changes, but they never seem to happen. This week, think about something in your life that you would like to be different. Is there a way that you can implement some simple steps toward this? If yes, go for it! If not, consider what is holding you back and what you could do to shift this.

JUN 17 – JUN 23
change

17 / MONDAY	18 / TUESDAY	19 / WEDNESDAY

NOTES

> "A ... difficult passage has prefaced
> every page I have turned in life."

CHARLOTTE BRONTË (1816–1855), ENGLISH NOVELIST

20 / THURSDAY
Summer Solstice (UK, ROI, CAN, USA)

21 / FRIDAY ♋
Winter Solstice (AUS, NZ)

22 / SATURDAY ○

23 / SUNDAY

EMBRACE THE UNEXPECTED

Sometimes in life we get hit with unexpected changes. This week, think about a recent change that has surprised you. How did you deal with it? Are you at peace with it now? And were you able to learn from it? Allow your answers to inspire you the next time you're going through a period of tricky change.

JUN 24 – JUN 30
change

24 / MONDAY
Whit Monday (Orthodox)

25 / TUESDAY

26 / WEDNESDAY

NOTES

> "Yesterday I was clever, so I wanted to change the world. Today I am wise, so I am changing myself."

RUMI (1207–1273), PERSIAN POET

27 / THURSDAY   28 / FRIDAY ☾   29/ SATURDAY

_____   _____   _____
_____   _____   _____
_____   _____   _____
_____   _____   _____
_____   _____   30 / SUNDAY
_____   _____   _____
_____   _____   _____
_____   _____   _____
_____   _____   _____

REFLECT ON YOUR GROWTH

This week, think about the "you" that you were
ten years ago. Consider whether you have
changed on an emotional level, and if these
changes are positive. Try to remember how you
felt at the time of each change. Emotional growth
is only possible due to change, so it's important to
remember this when things feel difficult.

JUNE OVERVIEW

M	TU	W	TH	F	SA	SU
27	28	29	30	31	1	2
3	4	5	6	7	8	9
10	11	12	13	14	15	1
17	18	19	20	21	22	23
24	25	26	27	28	29	30

This month I am grateful for . . .

_____

_____

_____

_____

_____

_____

_____

REFLECTIONS ON CHANGE

How has it felt to focus on the theme of change this month? Has it led you to recognize anything new about yourself and how you have grown over the years?

How have you coped with any changes over the last month in comparison to how you normally do?

In what ways will you try to embrace change more in the future?

JULY

CREATIVITY

Creativity is sometimes thought to only be relevant to people with a particular talent for some aspect of the arts. But in reality, creativity comes in all shapes and forms, which means we all have the ability to create anytime we want to.

Whether it's something specific, such as baking a cake or painting a picture, or something broader, such as considering how you can build a life that really works for you, creativity is accessible to each of us every single day!

Recognizing and embracing our innate ability to create is a special thing, as it helps us to express our authentic selves and develop a deeper sense of self-connection, self-confidence and personal freedom.

So, this month, take some time to think about what you would most like to express and create in life. My hope is that the weekly prompts in the pages that follow will help you with this, empowering you to curate a life that makes the most of your infinite creative potential.

AFFIRMATION OF THE MONTH

I am creating a life that works for me — one that I love and enjoy

JUL 1 – JUL 7
CREATIVITY

1 / MONDAY	2 / TUESDAY	3 / WEDNESDAY

NOTES

> "The creative mind is the playful mind."

ERIC HOFFER (1902–1983), AMERICAN PHILOSOPHER

4 / THURSDAY
Independence Day (USA)

5 / FRIDAY ●

6 / SATURDAY

7 / SUNDAY
Islamic New Year (first day of Muharram) begins at sundown

RECONNECT WITH YOUR INNER CHILD

As children, we are constantly using our imaginations to come up with all kinds of fun scenarios and activities. This week, think of something you loved to do as a child – perhaps drawing, singing or putting on shows. Then spend some time indulging in this creative pursuit, whether on your own or with friends.

JUL 8 – JUL 14
CREATIVITY

8 / MONDAY	9 / TUESDAY	10 / WEDNESDAY

NOTES

> "For it is only in freedom that we
> can be creative and so be happy."

KRISHNAMURTI (1895–1986), INDIAN PHILOSOPHER

11 / THURSDAY

12 / FRIDAY
Orangemen's Day (NIR)
Battle of the Boyne (NI)

13 / SATURDAY ☽

14 / SUNDAY

CREATE TIME FOR YOURSELF

Do you feel like you don't have enough time
to be creative? This week, adjust your schedule
to make time for something creative, even if
it's just for 15 minutes. Whether it's gardening,
dancing like no one's watching or writing a
short story – or whatever else you fancy – you
deserve some time to express yourself.

JUL 15 – JUL 21
CREATIVITY

15 / MONDAY	16 / TUESDAY	17 / WEDNESDAY

NOTES

> "Go confidently in the direction of your dreams! Live the life you've imagined."

HENRY DAVID THOREAU (1817–1862), AMERICAN WRITER AND PHILOSOPHER

18 / THURSDAY

19 / FRIDAY

20 / SATURDAY

21 / SUNDAY ○

BRING YOUR CREATIVE DREAMS TO LIFE

Have you always dreamed of learning a language? Becoming a better cook? Writing a book? Travelling the world? This week, make a list of all your creative dreams. Look into how you can start one of them this week. It's time to turn your dreams into a reality!

JUL 22 – JUL 28
CREATIVITY

22 / MONDAY ♌	23 / TUESDAY	24 / WEDNESDAY

NOTES

> "Normality is a paved road: it's comfortable to walk, but no flowers grow on it."
>
> VINCENT VAN GOGH (1853–1890), DUTCH PAINTER

25 / THURSDAY

26 / FRIDAY

27 / SATURDAY

28 / SUNDAY ☾

CREATE NEW CULINARY EXPERIENCES

Often we end up cooking the same things week in, week out – out of habit, comfort or lack of time and energy. This week, instead of cooking the same old meals, get creative in the kitchen by trying at least two new recipes. If you're not a fan of cooking, visit a new cafe or restaurant, or choose a takeaway you normally wouldn't.

JULY OVERVIEW

M	TU	W	TH	F	SA	SU
1	2	3	4	5	6	7
8	9	10	11	12	13	14
15	16	17	18	19	20	21
22	23	24	25	26	27	28
29	30	31	1	2	3	4

This month I am grateful for . . .

_____
_____
_____
_____
_____
_____
_____

REFLECTIONS ON CREATIVITY

In what ways have you tried to be more creative this month?

How has focusing on the theme of creativity this month made you feel?

Would you like to devote more time to creative pursuits in the future? If so, how can you make this happen?

LOVE

The world can feel like a heavy place at times, but love – in its many forms – almost always makes everything feel lighter and better.

Whether in the context of family, friendships, romantic relationships or our own passions, such as for nature, music, certain flavours and scents, or whatever else, love is a powerful thing. A life filled with love is one filled with joy, purpose and connection, helping us to feel less lonely when things get tough.

To love and feel loved gives us a sense of grounding and belonging – a safe harbour from the trials and tribulations of life. But to love and open ourselves to love is not always easy, especially if we've been let down or hurt in the past, as it can make us feel exposed and vulnerable.

The risk is, nonetheless, usually worth taking, as it makes our journey through life so much more heartening, fulfilling and exhilarating. So, this month, let's focus on bringing more love into our lives in any ways we can.

AFFIRMATION OF THE MONTH

My heart is open to both giving and receiving love

JUL 29 – AUG 4
LOVE

29 / MONDAY

30 / TUESDAY

31 / WEDNESDAY
Lughnasadh (Lammas)

NOTES

> "The more I bathe in the experience of loving and being loved, the more accessible it becomes in daily life."

TARA BRACH (1953–PRESENT), AMERICAN MEDITATION TEACHER

1 / THURSDAY	2 / FRIDAY	3 / SATURDAY
		4 / SUNDAY ●

IDENTIFY WHAT YOU LOVE

Love comes in many forms. This week, think about things that give you a warm, loving feeling – people, places, activities or events. Make a note of these so that you can incorporate more of them into your life. Consider why these things might make you feel so good. Do they have anything in common?

AUG 5 – AUG 11
LOVE

5 / MONDAY
August Bank Holiday
 (ROI, SCO)
Public Holiday (NSW, NT)

6 / TUESDAY

7 / WEDNESDAY

NOTES

> ## "There can be few greater gifts than to find oneself truly loved."

DEREK FROST (1952–PRESENT), FOUNDER OF AIDSARK

8 / THURSDAY

9 / FRIDAY

10 / SATURDAY

11 / SUNDAY

SPREAD THE LOVE

Showing love to others is one of the best ways to create a kinder, more loving society. So, every day this week, complete at least one small act of kindness for someone else. Hold open a door, give a compliment, treat someone to a coffee ... no matter how small you think the gesture is, it could make the world of difference to their day.

AUG 12 – AUG 18
LOVE

12 / MONDAY ☽	13 / TUESDAY	14 / WEDNESDAY

NOTES

> ## "One word frees us of all the weight and pain of life. That word is love."

SOPHOCLES (c. 496–406 BCE), ANCIENT GREEK PLAYWRIGHT

15 / THURSDAY

16 / FRIDAY

17 / SATURDAY

18 / SUNDAY

WRITE LOVE LETTERS

It's important to express your love, rather than bottling it up. This week, think about someone you love deeply. When was the last time you told them how much they mean to you? Write them a letter, telling them everything that makes them special. You don't have to send it – it's just good to let the love flow freely.

AUG 19 – AUG 25
LOVE

19 / MONDAY ○	20 / TUESDAY	21 / WEDNESDAY

NOTES

> "Every one of us needs to show how much we care for each other and, in the process, care for ourselves."

DIANA (1961–1997), PRINCESS OF WALES

22 / THURSDAY

23 / FRIDAY ♍

24 / SATURDAY

25 / SUNDAY

PRACTISE SELF-LOVE

Being loving toward ourselves can often feel more difficult than being loving toward others. This week, turn to the Inspired Journalling section at the back of the diary and make a list of things you love about yourself. It might feel tricky at first, but you can refer back to it when you need reminding of your many good qualities.

AUGUST OVERVIEW

M	TU	W	TH	F	SA	SU
29	30	31	1	2	3	4
5	6	7	8	9	10	11
12	13	14	15	16	17	18
19	20	21	22	23	24	25
26	27	28	29	30	31	1

This month I am grateful for . . .

REFLECTIONS ON LOVE

In what ways have you opened up to more love in your life this month?

_____

_____

_____

_____

_____

_____

How has focusing more on love this month made you feel?

_____

_____

_____

_____

_____

In what ways would you like to bring more love into your life in the future?

_____

_____

_____

_____

_____

SEPTEMBER

COURAGE

Being courageous involves having the strength
and willingness to venture forward with something even in
the face of difficulty, fear, pain or sometimes danger.
It can be found in both quiet, everyday moments and
in bigger, more dramatic events.

There can be great courage in just getting out of bed
in the morning when your body is feeling heavy with
sadness; in speaking up when your stomach is churning
with nerves; or in taking a step that you know is right,
despite being unsure of what's going to come next.

Whether big or small, every act of courage deserves
recognition. So, this month, let's shine a spotlight on the
theme of courage by recognizing the ways in which we're
already putting it into practice, as well as by exploring
more ways in which we can harness it to stop our fears
from holding us back in life!

AFFIRMATION OF THE MONTH

I inhale courage
and exhale fear

AUG 26 – SEP 1
COURAGE

26 / MONDAY ☾
Summer Bank Holiday
(UK, except SCO)

27 / TUESDAY

28 / WEDNESDAY

NOTES

> "The brave man is not he who does not feel afraid, but he who conquers that fear."

NELSON MANDELA (1918–2013), SOUTH AFRICAN PRESIDENT

29 / THURSDAY

30 / FRIDAY

31 / SATURDAY

1 / SUNDAY
Father's Day (AUS, NZ)

FIND YOUR COURAGE

When we fear something, we often put off doing it. Unfortunately, this usually results in it feeling like a bigger deal. This week, take time to identify one thing that you've been putting off and figure out what steps you can take to tackle it head-on. There's no time like the present to find your ever-accessible courage.

SEP 2 – SEP 8
COURAGE

2 / MONDAY
Labour Day (CAN, USA)

3 / TUESDAY ●

4 / WEDNESDAY

NOTES

> ## "Life shrinks or expands in proportion to one's courage."
>
> ANAÏS NIN (1903–1977), FRENCH AUTHOR

5 / THURSDAY   6 / FRIDAY   7 / SATURDAY

------------   ------------   ------------
------------   ------------   ------------
------------   ------------   ------------
------------   ------------
------------   ------------   8 / SUNDAY
------------   ------------   ------------
------------   ------------   ------------
------------   ------------   ------------
------------   ------------   ------------
------------   ------------   ------------

CELEBRATE YOUR COURAGE

It's important to recognize your inner reserves
of courage each time you draw from them – to
keep replenishing them. This week, look out for
all the ways, big or small, in which you exercise
bravery on a day-to-day basis. And celebrate
these! Give yourself a pat on the back. You
deserve to feel proud.

SEP 9 – SEP 15
COURAGE

9 / MONDAY	10 / TUESDAY	11 / WEDNESDAY ☽

NOTES

> "Above all, be the heroine of
> your life, not the victim."

NORA EPHRON (1941–2012), AMERICAN WRITER AND FILMMAKER

12 / THURSDAY

13 / FRIDAY

14 / SATURDAY

15 / SUNDAY
Milad un-Nabi (birthday of
the Prophet Muhammed)
begins at sundown

REMEMBER YOUR COURAGE

We face many challenges throughout our lives,
but we can easily forget what we have faced
and achieved. This week, turn to the Inspired
Journalling section at the back of the diary and
make a list of times when bravery has got you
through. The next time you have a wobble, look
at the list as a reminder of your inner strength.

SEP 16 – SEP 22
COURAGE

16 / MONDAY

17 / TUESDAY

18 / WEDNESDAY ○

NOTES

> ## "Efforts and courage are not enough
> ## without purpose and direction."

JOHN F. KENNEDY (1917–1963), 35TH AMERICAN PRESIDENT

19 / THURSDAY	20 / FRIDAY	21 / SATURDAY
		International Day of Peace

22 / SUNDAY
Autumn Equinox
(UK, ROI, CAN, USA)
Spring Equinox (AUS, NZ)

TAKE TIME OUT

Life's ups and downs can leave us feeling a little
worn out. And it can take courage to admit this!
This week, be brave enough to devote some time
to self-care. Whether taking a bath, going for
a walk in nature or arranging a therapy session,
give yourself whatever you need to replenish
your stores of energy, resilience and courage!

SEP 23 – SEP 29
COURAGE

23 / MONDAY ♎   24 / TUESDAY ☾   25 / WEDNESDAY

NOTES

> "My courage always rises at
> every attempt to intimidate me."

JANE AUSTEN (1775–1817), ENGLISH NOVELIST

26 / THURSDAY

27 / FRIDAY

28 / SATURDAY

29 / SUNDAY

ADDRESS YOUR FEARS

Our fears can sometimes seems like a shadow
looming over us. This week, imagine this shadow
as a person looking over your shoulder, making
you feel worried and intimidated. What would
you like to say to them? Write a letter, explaining
how they affect you, and remind yourself that
you are capable of standing up to them.

SEPTEMBER OVERVIEW

M	TU	W	TH	F	SA	SU
26	27	28	29	30	31	1
2	3	4	5	6	7	8
9	10	11	12	13	14	15
16	17	18	19	20	21	22
23	24	25	26	27	28	29
30	1	2	3	4	5	6

This month I am grateful for . . .

REFLECTIONS ON COURAGE

In what ways have you been able to recognize and tap into your own reserves of courage this month?

How did it feel to explore and celebrate what courage feels and looks like for you?

Are there any ways you'd like to develop your courage more in the future?

OCTOBER

NURTURING

When going about our busy daily lives, we're often required to take care of and "nurture" many different people and things all at once – whether family, friends, neighbours, colleagues, pets, plants or work projects.

But have you ever stopped to think about whether you're truly giving yourself the care that you need and deserve – by nurturing your thought patterns, your mind, your passions and your cherished relationships?

Looking after others and their needs is, of course, important. But if we don't tend to our own needs, nurture our own souls and help ourselves develop and grow stronger, looking after others can become incredibly difficult, as we can feel like we're running on empty!

My hope is that this month's weekly prompts will help you to become more familiar with what a sense of nurturing looks and feels like for you, so that you can connect more with your inner nurturer, learn how to recharge your batteries and never have to run on empty again!

AFFIRMATION OF THE MONTH

I take daily steps to nurture
my body, mind and soul

SEP 30 – OCT 6
NURTURING

30 / MONDAY

1 / TUESDAY
Black History Month
begins (UK)

2 / WEDNESDAY ●
Rosh Hashanah (Jewish New
Year) begins at sundown

NOTES

> "Nurture your mind with great thoughts.
> To believe in the heroic makes heroes."

BENJAMIN DISRAELI (1804–1881), BRITISH PRIME MINISTER

3 / THURSDAY

4 / FRIDAY

5 / SATURDAY

6 / SUNDAY

NURTURE YOUR HEADSPACE

What are your biggest worries right now? This week, sit down with some paper and do a brain dump of all the anxiety-inducing things that are taking up valuable headspace. Then throw the paper away, gently telling yourself that it's okay to let go of your worries and to focus on the *nurturing* things in life instead.

OCT 7 – OCT 13
NURTURING

7 / MONDAY
Public Holiday
(ACT, NSW, QLD, SA)

_____

_____

_____

_____

_____

_____

_____

_____

_____

_____

_____

8 / TUESDAY

_____

_____

_____

_____

_____

_____

_____

_____

_____

_____

_____

9 / WEDNESDAY

_____

_____

_____

_____

_____

_____

_____

_____

_____

_____

_____

NOTES

_____

_____

_____

> "Self-love is choosing more positive and
> self-empowering thoughts ... which lead
> to more self-nurturing behaviour."

MEL COLLINS (1970–PRESENT), BRITISH SPIRITUAL LIFE COACH

10 / THURSDAY ☽

11 / FRIDAY
Yom Kippur (Day of
Atonement) begins
at sundown

12 / SATURDAY

13 / SUNDAY

THINK NURTURING THOUGHTS

Our internal voices can say the harshest things.
This week, try to be more mindful of the voice
in your head. When it says something negative,
reframe it. For example, you might change "I
hate that I'm so sensitive" to "My sensitivity is a
strength that allows me to connect with people
on a deeper level, and I'm grateful for that".

OCT 14 – OCT 20
NURTURING

14 / MONDAY
Thanksgiving (CAN)
Indigenous Peoples' Day/
Columbus Day

15 / TUESDAY

16 / WEDNESDAY
Sukkot (Feast of the
Tabernacles) begins
at sundown

NOTES

> "Always be on the lookout for
> ways to nurture your dream."

LAO TZU (6TH CENTURY BCE), CHINESE PHILOSOPHER

17 / THURSDAY ○ 　　**18 / FRIDAY** 　　**19 / SATURDAY**

_____ 　 _____ 　 _____
_____ 　 _____ 　 _____
_____ 　 _____ 　 _____
_____ 　 _____ 　 _____
_____ 　 _____ 　 **20 / SUNDAY**
_____ 　 _____ 　 _____
_____ 　 _____ 　 _____
_____ 　 _____ 　 _____
_____ 　 _____ 　 _____

NURTURE YOUR PASSIONS

What activities in life nourish you, revitalize
you and make you feel like you're lighting up
from the inside? Write down five things that
you can refer to next time you're having a hard
day. Whether it's dancing, reading, listening to
music or something else, aim to indulge in one
of your passions at least three times this week.

OCT 21 – OCT 27
NURTURING

21 / MONDAY	22 / TUESDAY	23 / WEDNESDAY ♏

NOTES

> "When we nurture our own happiness,
> we nurture other people's happiness."

TEAL SWAN (1984-PRESENT), AMERICAN SPIRITUAL INFLUENCER

24 / THURSDAY ☾   25 / FRIDAY   26 / SATURDAY

----------------   ----------------   ----------------

----------------   ----------------   ----------------

----------------   ----------------   ----------------

----------------   ----------------   27 / SUNDAY
                                             British Summer Time ends
----------------   ----------------   ----------------

----------------   ----------------   ----------------

----------------   ----------------   ----------------

----------------   ----------------   ----------------

NURTURE YOUR RELATIONSHIPS

Who do you cherish most in your life? And
who makes you feel the most cherished? This
week, reach out to these people and spend some
mutually nurturing time with them. Whether
it is a date night with a partner, coffee with a
friend or a phone call with a family member,
soak up the feeling and let it feed your soul.

OCTOBER OVERVIEW

M	TU	W	TH	F	SA	SU
30	1	2	3	4	5	6
7	8	9	10	11	12	13
14	15	16	17	18	19	20
21	22	23	24	25	26	27
28	29	30	31	1	2	3

This month I am grateful for . . .

_____

_____

_____

_____

_____

_____

REFLECTIONS ON NURTURING

In what ways have you managed to bring more of a sense of nurturing into your life this month?

How has focusing on nurturing your own needs made you feel?

In what ways do you think looking after your own needs more will help you in the future?

Don't miss out on next year's diary! See the back page for details on how to order your copy

NOVEMBER

LEARNING

Learning is viewed by some people as something that can only happen in a classroom. But, whether we realize it or not, we all have the capacity to learn constantly as we move through life. It's only by embracing this that we'll be able to adapt to life's inevitable changes.

Every experience that we have carries the potential to better equip us for future scenarios if we can pause and consider how we might learn from it.

Sometimes we learn and adjust without even making a conscious decision. But often we have to make a conscious effort to find the useful lessons in our daily lives – especially if our experiences seem "bad" at the time, such as getting into an argument, or losing something valuable.

It's always worth making the effort to learn, though, as with learning comes growth, and with growth comes a deeper sense of accomplishment and fulfilment.

My hope is that this month's weekly prompts will help you adopt more of an attitude of openness and learning in everything you do.

AFFIRMATION OF THE MONTH

I am continually open to learning, evolving and growing

OCT 28 – NOV 3
LEARNING

28 / MONDAY
Labour Day (NZ)

29 / TUESDAY

30 / WEDNESDAY

NOTES

> "The adventure of life is to learn. The purpose of life is to grow ... The secret of life is to dare."

WILLIAM ARTHUR WARD (1921–1994), AMERICAN WRITER

31 / THURSDAY
Halloween
Samhain

1 / FRIDAY ●
All Saints' Day
Diwali

2 / SATURDAY
All Souls' Day

------

3 / SUNDAY
Daylight Saving Time ends
(CAN, USA)

EXPAND YOUR VIEWS

Experiencing new things teaches us to be more
flexible and open. This week, expose yourself to
something new: this might be a conversation
with someone whose opinions differ from yours
or a news source that challenges your viewpoint.
Lean into this experience and identify at least
one thing that you can take away from it.

NOV 4 – NOV 10
LEARNING

4 / MONDAY	5 / TUESDAY	6 / WEDNESDAY
	Guy Fawkes Day	

NOTES

> "In the beginner's mind there are many possibilities, but in the expert's, there are few."

SHUNRYU SUZUKI (1904–1971), SOTO ZEN MONK AND TEACHER

7 / THURSDAY

8 / FRIDAY

9 / SATURDAY ☽

10 / SUNDAY

ADOPT A BEGINNER'S MINDSET

This week, set aside some time to learn more about something you love. Whether it be playing the piano, growing herbs or meditating, immerse yourself in your learning by approaching it without preconceptions or expectations. Discover how much lighter adopting this kind of beginner's mindset makes you feel.

NOV 11 – NOV 17
LEARNING

11 / MONDAY
Veterans Day (USA)
Remembrance Day (CAN, UK)

12 / TUESDAY

13 / WEDNESDAY

NOTES

> "In my life, I have found two things of priceless worth – learning and loving."

ARTHUR C. CLARKE (1917–2008), ENGLISH FUTURIST AND WRITER

14 / THURSDAY
King's birthday

15 / FRIDAY ○

16 / SATURDAY

_____

_____

_____

_____

_____

17 / SUNDAY

_____

_____

_____

_____

_____

WRITE TO YOUR YOUNGER SELF

Growing up often feels messy. This week, turn
to the Inspired Journalling section at the back of
the diary and think of a time when you remember
feeling lost. Write a letter of reassurance to your
younger self, expressing that although this time
feels tough, you will get through it and everything
that you learn from it will lead to good places.

NOV 18 – NOV 24
LEARNING

18 / MONDAY	19 / TUESDAY	20 / WEDNESDAY

NOTES

> "When any real progress is made, we unlearn and learn anew what we thought we knew before."

HENRY DAVID THOREAU (1817–1862), AMERICAN NATURALIST

21 / THURSDAY
World Hello Day

22 / FRIDAY ♐

23 / SATURDAY ☾

24 / SUNDAY

EMBRACE "UNLEARNING"

Sometimes things we have learned in the past can become outdated. It's important to be willing to "unlearn" old habits and replace them with new ways of doing or being. This week, identify one area of your life where you could benefit from learning new approaches, whether on your own or with the help of others.

NOVEMBER OVERVIEW

M	TU	W	TH	F	SA	SU
28	29	30	31	1	2	3
4	5	6	7	8	9	10
11	12	13	14	15	16	17
18	19	20	21	22	23	24
25	26	27	28	29	30	1

This month I am grateful for . . .

REFLECTIONS ON LEARNING

How have you found focusing on learning more this month?

What are the most valuable lessons that you have learned?

In what ways would you like to continue to embrace an attitude of continual learning in the future?

DECEMBER

SELF-REFLECTION

Taking regular time out to mindfully reflect on how we're choosing to lead our lives gives us the opportunity to get to know ourselves better – our thoughts, beliefs, wants, needs, emotions, behaviours and motivations.

Such self-reflection, and the resulting self-knowledge, can give us a much-needed sense of perspective in our lives, and help us decide if we'd like to make any changes for the better.

As we now approach the end of the year, let's take another opportunity to self-reflect. My hope is that the weekly prompts on the pages that follow will encourage you to take an honest look in the mirror and, as a result, live a more balanced, deliberately authentic and happy life.

AFFIRMATION OF THE MONTH

Making time for regular self-reflection deepens my connection with both myself and the world around me

NOV 25 – DEC 1
SELF-REFLECTION

25 / MONDAY	26 / TUESDAY	27 / WEDNESDAY

NOTES

> ## "The unexamined life is not worth living."
>
> SOCRATES (c. 470–399 BCE), GREEK PHILOSOPHER

28 / THURSDAY
Thanksgiving (USA)

29 / FRIDAY

30 / SATURDAY
St Andrew's Day

1 / SUNDAY ●
World AIDS Day
First Sunday of Advent

REFLECT ON PAST CHOICES

We've all encountered situations that we wish we had handled differently – with more grace, humility, confidence or compassion. This week, choose one past scenario and reflect on why you think you behaved the way you did. How could you handle it differently next time? And how might the result differ?

DEC 2 – DEC 8
SELF-REFLECTION

2 / MONDAY
St Andrew's Day observed
(SCO)

3 / TUESDAY

4 / WEDNESDAY

NOTES

> "Within you, there is a stillness and sanctuary to which you can retreat at any time and be yourself."

HERMANN HESSE (1877–1962), GERMAN-BORN SWISS AUTHOR

5 / THURSDAY   6 / FRIDAY   7 / SATURDAY

_____   _____   _____
_____   _____   _____
_____   _____   _____
_____   _____   _____
_____   _____   8 / SUNDAY ☽
_____   _____   _____
_____   _____   _____
_____   _____   _____
_____   _____   _____
_____   _____   _____

CHECK IN REGULARLY

We can be so busy dwelling on the past or looking to the future that we can forget to reflect on where we are right now. This week, take a few moments each day to check in with how you are feeling – tired, frustrated, calm or grounded? If there's discomfort, what could you do to change this? Or might it be best to let it pass?

DEC 9 – DEC 15
SELF-REFLECTION

9 / MONDAY	10 / TUESDAY	11 / WEDNESDAY

NOTES

> "The privilege of a lifetime is to become who you truly are."

CARL GUSTAV JUNG (1875–1961), SWISS PSYCHIATRIST

12 / THURSDAY   13 / FRIDAY   14 / SATURDAY

_____   _____   _____
_____   _____   _____
_____   _____   _____
_____   _____   _____
_____   _____   15 / SUNDAY ○
_____   _____   _____
_____   _____   _____
_____   _____   _____
_____   _____   _____
_____   _____   _____

DESCRIBE YOUR IDEAL SELF

This week, reflect on which words describe you as you are right now and write down ten of them. Then write down ten words that you'd ideally _like_ to use to describe yourself. How many of these align? And for those that don't, how could you adjust things in your life so that more of them are in alignment?

DEC 16 – DEC 22
SELF-REFLECTION

16 / MONDAY

17 / TUESDAY

18 / WEDNESDAY

NOTES

> "Passion is energy. Feel the power that comes from focusing on what excites you."

OPRAH WINFREY (1954–PRESENT), AMERICAN TV HOST

19 / THURSDAY   20 / FRIDAY   21 / SATURDAY ♑

22 / SUNDAY ☾

ADVOCATE FOR YOUR ENERGY

This week, think about what you spend most (and least) energy on. Then draw a pie chart to show this visually. Are you happy with the balance? If not, draw how you would like your chart to look in an ideal world and start taking steps toward rebalancing things.

DEC 23 – DEC 29
SELF-REFLECTION

23 / MONDAY

24 / TUESDAY
Christmas Eve

25 / WEDNESDAY
Christmas Day
Hanukkah begins at sundown

NOTES

> "One of the most sincere forms of respect is actually listening to what another has to say."

BRYANT H. MCGILL (1969–PRESENT), AMERICAN SOCIAL ENTREPRENEUR

26 / THURSDAY
Boxing Day
St Stephen's Day
Kwanzaa begins

27 / FRIDAY

28 / SATURDAY

29 / SUNDAY

REFLECT ON YOUR COMMUNICATION

How we connect with the people around us is fundamental to our quality of life. This week, reflect on your talking and listening skills. How could you open up more and communicate better? Do you listen to what others say, or do you just wait for your chance to talk? If the latter, how can you change this?

DEC 30 – JAN 5
SELF-REFLECTION

30 / MONDAY ●

31 / TUESDAY
New Year's Eve

1 / WEDNESDAY
New Year's Day
Kwanzaa ends

NOTES

> You have to dream before your
> dreams can come true."

A. P. J. ABDUL KALAM (1931–2015), 11TH PRESIDENT OF INDIA

2 / THURSDAY
Hanukkah ends at sundown

3 / FRIDAY

4 / SATURDAY

5 / SUNDAY

TUNE IN TO YOUR DREAMS

Reflecting on our innermost wishes and dreams
is a wonderful way of checking whether we're
currently on the right path. This week, lean into
three things that you'd ultimately like to achieve
in life. Then consider how you can start to work
toward these dreams and clearly write down
your intentions in this regard.

DECEMBER OVERVIEW

M	TU	W	TH	F	SA	SU
25	26	27	28	29	**30**	1
2	3	4	5	6	7	8
9	10	11	12	13	14	15
16	17	18	19	20	21	22
23	24	25	26	27	28	29
30	31	1	2	3	4	5

This month I am grateful for . . .

_____

_____

_____

_____

_____

_____

REFLECTIONS ON SELF-REFLECTION

How have you found focusing on the theme of self-reflection this month?

Do you feel like you know yourself a little better now than at the start of the month, and do have any better an understanding of what you want in life?

In what ways do you think self-reflection will continue to help you in the year to come?

INSPIRED
JOURNALLING

The journalling pages that follow will encourage you to spend
a little time reflecting on some of the fundamentals in life,
which I shop will help you feel grateful, grounded, motivated,
connected, resilient and comforted throughout the year.

Each of the six pages corresponds to one of the monthly
themes in the main diary and gives you space to create a
personalized list or helpful note – of things that you are
grateful for, what helps you to feel peaceful, places you'd like
to visit, things that you love about yourself, times you have
shown courage and reassurances for your younger self.

Feel free to write as much or as little as you want for each
theme – there's no right or wrong here. And feel free
to then come back to these pages, add to them or draw
strength from them, anytime it's helpful for you.

Things that I'm Grateful for

HOPE (FEBRUARY)

Spending time reflecting on the things that we're grateful for is a wonderful way to restore our hope if ever we are feeling low, uncertain or distressed. Honing in on what enhances our lives and fills us up emotionally can also offer us a useful reminder of what to look to improve in our lives – in order to start feeling even more positive and hopeful.

Use the space below to compile a list of all the things that you are grateful for in your life. What makes you feel happy, whole and contented? You can then refer back to this list anytime you need reminding of the many good things in your life.

what helps me feel peaceful

PEACE (MARCH)

We're often so busy rushing about from one job to the next in life that we don't stop to give ourselves the rest and relaxation that we need and deserve. Knowing some specific activities that help us to feel more peaceful is key for our wellbeing, as it gives us tools to recharge our batteries when it's most needed.

With this in mind, use the space below to make a list of activities that bring you a sense of peace, contentment and relaxation. This could include anything from listening to music, cooking and watching your favourite TV show to walking, dancing or going on a run that clears your head. Once you've made the list, you can refer back to it if ever you need some valuable chill time.

places I would like to visit

ADVENTURE (APRIL)

Travelling, whether to destinations near or far, is a wonderful way to feed your adventurous spirit – or help to bring it out. Whether visiting a local museum, a new local garden or an entirely different country, travel helps us to stay curious and broaden our view on things.

While it would be impossible to go on big outings and far-flung trips every week, there is no harm in making a list of ideas for the times when you can. So, take a moment to think about all the places you'd ideally like to go and pop them in a list below. Near, far, big or small, add them all. And then come back to this list if, at any point, you have a window of time and feel the urge to reignite your sense of adventure in life.

Things I Love about Myself

LOVE (AUGUST)

The voice of our inner critic can be incredibly mean and persistent, continually pointing out our perceived flaws and "negatives". So, it can be super useful to counteract it at times by showing yourself the kind of love that you're probably more used to showering on others.

With this in mind, use the space below to write a list of all the things that you like or ,even better, love about yourself. It can be anything at all – from personal qualities like generosity or empathy, to things that you have achieved and ways that you have helped others. Use the creation of this list to celebrate everything "you", and then refer back to it anytime you need a little confidence boost.

Times I have shown courage

COURAGE (SEPTEMBER)

You've made it through every difficult experience in your life up to this moment! Yet we often don't take the time to stop and congratulate ourselves for this. You deserve to feel proud of all that you've faced and overcome up until now, instead of just overlooking it and moving on to the next hurdles that life throws your way.

With this in mind, take a moment to think about all the times that your courage has got you through challenges or difficulties. Write these down in the space below. They might be big or small – getting through break-ups, fall-outs, rejections, bereavements, moving house, starting new jobs, having a new baby … anything goes! You can then look back at this list anytime you need a reminder of how incredibly strong and resilient you really are.

A Letter of Reassurance to My younger self

LEARNING (NOVEMBER)

Life is full of trials and tribulations, ups and downs, woes as well as joys … and this can take a bit of getting used to as we're growing up and taking on the responsibilities of adulthood. It can be a steep learning curve at times!

With this in mind, think back to a time in your younger years when things felt particularly tough or confusing, and take this chance to write a letter in the space below to this younger, less experienced version of yourself, reassuring them that everything is going to be okay. What words of support can you offer to let yourself know that all the learning you are going through now will be worth it in the end?

Although it might feel tough to write this letter, it gives you the valuable opportunity to recognize just how much you have learned and grown over the years – and to give yourself a pat on the back for having become the version of yourself that you are today.

Notes from the Author

Hello, I'm Jess – a designer, illustrator and writer based in West Yorkshire, UK.

I run my Instagram page @jessrachelsharp, where I share gentle, positive reminders for when you might need them most. I also have my own line of stationery, enamel pins and gifts, which I sell from my website: www.jessrachelsharp.com. My hope is that my products can offer some support and encouragement through life's many ups and downs.

I began doing what I do after going through a bit of a tough time and attending therapy. I wanted to remember all the helpful words that I was hearing and life-enhancing epiphanies that I was having, so I began to incorporate them into designs. I started posting them to my Instagram and I realized that not only were they helpful for me, but they resonated with others, too. And I haven't stopped since!

It has been an absolute dream to work with Watkins Publishing on putting these ideas into this diary. I hope you find it as uplifting and inspiring to read and use as I have found it to create.

We are constantly learning and growing on our journey through life, so I hope that this diary can offer some gentle guidance for you along the way – helping you to discover more about yourself and make the very most of each and every day.

Here's wishing you much love, hope and happiness for a fulfilling year ahead!

Jess xxx

Notes

Don't miss out on next year's diary!

To pre-order your 2025 *Every Day Matters Diary*
with FREE postage and packing*
call our UK distributor on +44 (0)1206 255800.

*Free postage and packing for UK delivery addresses only. Offer limited to three books per order.

WATKINS
Sharing Wisdom
Since 1893

Our books celebrate conscious, passionate, wise and happy living.
Be part of the community by visiting
watkinspublishing.com

WatkinsPublishing
WatkinsPublishingLtd

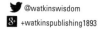

@watkinswisdom
+watkinspublishing1893